50 Delicious Premium Roast Dishes

By: Kelly Johnson

Table of Contents

- Prime Rib Roast
- Herb-Crusted Rack of Lamb
- Garlic Butter Beef Tenderloin
- Porchetta (Italian-Style Pork Roast)
- Honey Glazed Ham
- Moroccan Spiced Leg of Lamb
- Slow-Roasted Pork Belly
- Classic Roast Chicken
- Duck à l'Orange
- Bourbon Glazed Beef Brisket
- Cranberry-Stuffed Turkey Breast
- Korean BBQ Short Ribs
- Miso-Marinated Roast Salmon
- Peking Duck
- Maple Dijon Roasted Pork Loin
- Citrus-Herb Roasted Sea Bass
- Slow-Roasted Tomahawk Steak
- Char Siu (Chinese BBQ Pork)
- Coffee-Rubbed Prime Rib
- Mustard-Crusted Roast Lamb
- Balsamic Glazed Roast Quail
- Rosemary Garlic Roasted Venison
- Indian-Spiced Roast Goat
- Applewood Smoked Pork Shoulder
- Five-Spice Roasted Duck
- Chimichurri Roasted Tri-Tip
- Herb Butter Roasted Cornish Hen
- Tandoori Spiced Roast Chicken
- Szechuan Peppercorn Beef Roast
- Black Garlic Roasted Turkey
- Maple Bourbon Glazed Salmon
- Braised and Roasted Oxtail
- Cajun Spiced Roast Pork
- Brown Sugar Glazed Meatloaf
- Soy-Ginger Glazed Roast Goose

- French Onion Roasted Ribeye
- Roasted Bison Sirloin
- Pistachio Crusted Rack of Lamb
- Hoisin-Glazed Roast Duck
- Garlic Rosemary Roasted Wild Boar
- Argentine Asado Beef Roast
- Cherry Balsamic Glazed Roast Chicken
- Pomegranate Molasses Roasted Lamb
- Truffle Butter Roasted Filet Mignon
- Smoked Paprika Roasted Pork Ribs
- Lebanese Spiced Roast Leg of Lamb
- Harissa Roasted Chicken
- Plum-Glazed Roast Pheasant
- Saffron and Orange Roasted Quail
- Fig and Port Wine Roasted Venison

Perfect Prime Rib Roast

Ingredients:

- 1 (4-6 lb) bone-in prime rib roast
- 2 tbsp kosher salt
- 1 tbsp freshly ground black pepper
- 1 tbsp garlic powder
- 1 tbsp onion powder
- 1 tbsp fresh rosemary, finely chopped
- 1 tbsp fresh thyme, finely chopped
- 2 tbsp olive oil or softened butter

Instructions:

1. **Preparation:** Remove the roast from the refrigerator at least 2 hours before cooking to bring it to room temperature.
2. **Seasoning:** Pat the roast dry with paper towels. Mix salt, pepper, garlic powder, onion powder, rosemary, and thyme in a small bowl. Rub the roast all over with olive oil or butter, then coat evenly with the seasoning mixture.
3. **Preheat Oven:** Set the oven to 450°F (232°C).
4. **Initial Sear:** Place the roast bone-side down in a roasting pan with a rack. Roast for 15-20 minutes to develop a crust.
5. **Lower Temperature:** Reduce the oven temperature to 325°F (163°C) and continue roasting until the internal temperature reaches:
    - 120°F (49°C) for rare
    - 130°F (54°C) for medium-rare
    - 140°F (60°C) for medium
6. **Resting:** Remove the roast from the oven, tent it loosely with foil, and let it rest for at least 20-30 minutes before slicing. This allows the juices to redistribute.
7. **Serving:** Slice against the grain and serve with au jus or horseradish sauce.

Herb-Crusted Rack of Lamb

Ingredients:

- 1 (8-rib) rack of lamb, frenched
- 2 tbsp Dijon mustard
- 2 tbsp olive oil
- 3 cloves garlic, minced
- ½ cup breadcrumbs (panko or regular)
- 2 tbsp fresh rosemary, finely chopped
- 2 tbsp fresh thyme, finely chopped
- 1 tsp salt
- ½ tsp black pepper

Instructions:

1. Preheat oven to 400°F (200°C).
2. Season the lamb with salt and pepper. Sear in olive oil over medium-high heat until browned, about 2 minutes per side.
3. Brush the rack with Dijon mustard.
4. In a bowl, mix breadcrumbs, garlic, rosemary, thyme, and a little olive oil. Press the mixture onto the lamb.
5. Roast for 20-25 minutes or until internal temp reaches 125°F (52°C) for medium-rare.
6. Rest for 10 minutes, slice, and serve.

Garlic Butter Beef Tenderloin

Ingredients:

- 1 (3-4 lb) beef tenderloin, trimmed
- 2 tbsp olive oil
- 1 tbsp salt
- 1 tsp black pepper
- 4 tbsp butter, softened
- 4 cloves garlic, minced
- 1 tbsp fresh rosemary, chopped
- 1 tbsp fresh thyme, chopped

Instructions:

1. Preheat oven to 425°F (218°C).
2. Pat the tenderloin dry, season with salt and pepper.
3. Heat olive oil in a skillet and sear all sides until browned.
4. Mix butter, garlic, rosemary, and thyme. Spread over the tenderloin.
5. Roast for 20-25 minutes until the internal temp reaches 130°F (54°C) for medium-rare.
6. Let rest for 15 minutes before slicing.

Porchetta (Italian-Style Pork Roast)

Ingredients:

- 1 (4-5 lb) pork belly, skin-on
- 1 (2-3 lb) pork loin
- 1 tbsp salt
- 1 tsp black pepper
- 6 cloves garlic, minced
- 1 tbsp fennel seeds, toasted and crushed
- 1 tbsp rosemary, chopped
- 1 tbsp thyme, chopped
- 1 tbsp red pepper flakes (optional)
- Zest of 1 lemon
- 2 tbsp olive oil

Instructions:

1. Lay pork belly skin-side down. Season with salt, pepper, garlic, fennel, rosemary, thyme, red pepper flakes, and lemon zest.
2. Place the pork loin in the center and roll the belly tightly around it. Tie with butcher's twine.
3. Refrigerate uncovered overnight to dry out the skin.
4. Preheat oven to 300°F (150°C). Roast on a rack for 3-4 hours.
5. Increase heat to 450°F (232°C) for the last 30 minutes to crisp the skin.
6. Rest for 20 minutes before slicing.

Honey Glazed Ham

Ingredients:

- 1 (8-10 lb) bone-in ham, fully cooked
- 1 cup honey
- ½ cup brown sugar
- ¼ cup Dijon mustard
- 2 tbsp apple cider vinegar
- 1 tsp cinnamon
- ½ tsp cloves

Instructions:

1. Preheat oven to 325°F (163°C). Score the ham in a diamond pattern.
2. Wrap in foil and bake for about 1½ hours.
3. In a saucepan, combine honey, brown sugar, mustard, vinegar, cinnamon, and cloves. Simmer for 5 minutes.
4. Unwrap the ham and brush with the glaze.
5. Bake uncovered for another 30-40 minutes, basting every 10 minutes.
6. Rest for 15 minutes before slicing.

Moroccan Spiced Leg of Lamb

Ingredients:

- 1 (5-6 lb) bone-in leg of lamb
- 3 tbsp olive oil
- 4 cloves garlic, minced
- 2 tbsp ground cumin
- 2 tbsp ground coriander
- 1 tbsp ground cinnamon
- 1 tbsp smoked paprika
- 1 tsp ground ginger
- 1 tsp cayenne pepper
- 1 tbsp salt
- 1 tsp black pepper
- Juice of 1 lemon
- 2 tbsp honey

Instructions:

1. Mix olive oil, garlic, spices, lemon juice, and honey into a paste.
2. Rub all over the lamb and marinate for at least 4 hours or overnight.
3. Preheat oven to 325°F (163°C).
4. Roast for 2.5-3 hours, basting occasionally, until internal temp reaches 135°F (57°C) for medium-rare.
5. Rest for 15 minutes before slicing.

Slow-Roasted Pork Belly

Ingredients:

- 3 lb pork belly, skin-on
- 1 tbsp salt
- 1 tsp black pepper
- 1 tbsp Chinese five-spice powder
- 2 cloves garlic, minced
- 1 tbsp soy sauce
- 1 tbsp rice vinegar

Instructions:

1. Score the skin in a crosshatch pattern and rub with salt.
2. Mix spices, garlic, soy sauce, and vinegar and rub onto the meat (not the skin).
3. Refrigerate uncovered overnight.
4. Preheat oven to 300°F (150°C). Roast for 2.5-3 hours.
5. Increase heat to 450°F (232°C) for the last 30 minutes to crisp the skin.

Classic Roast Chicken

Ingredients:

- 1 whole chicken (4-5 lb)
- 2 tbsp olive oil or butter
- 1 tbsp salt
- 1 tsp black pepper
- 1 tsp paprika
- 1 tsp garlic powder
- 1 tsp onion powder
- 1 lemon, halved
- 4 cloves garlic, smashed
- 3 sprigs rosemary

Instructions:

1. Preheat oven to 425°F (218°C).
2. Pat chicken dry and rub with oil or butter.
3. Season with salt, pepper, paprika, garlic powder, and onion powder.
4. Stuff the cavity with lemon halves, garlic, and rosemary.
5. Roast for 1-1.5 hours, basting occasionally, until internal temp reaches 165°F (74°C).
6. Rest for 15 minutes before carving.

Duck à l'Orange

Ingredients:

- 1 whole duck (5-6 lb)
- 1 tbsp salt
- 1 tsp black pepper
- 1 orange, quartered
- 3 tbsp honey
- ½ cup orange juice
- ¼ cup white wine vinegar
- 1 cup chicken broth

Instructions:

1. Preheat oven to 375°F (190°C). Score duck skin and season with salt and pepper.
2. Stuff cavity with orange quarters.
3. Roast for 2-2.5 hours, basting occasionally.
4. In a saucepan, simmer honey, orange juice, vinegar, and broth until thickened.
5. Brush sauce onto the duck in the last 20 minutes of roasting.

Bourbon Glazed Beef Brisket

Ingredients:

- 1 (4-5 lb) beef brisket
- 2 tbsp salt
- 1 tbsp black pepper
- 1 tbsp smoked paprika
- 1 tbsp garlic powder
- 1 cup bourbon
- ½ cup brown sugar
- ¼ cup apple cider vinegar
- 1 cup beef broth

Instructions:

1. Preheat oven to 300°F (150°C).
2. Season brisket with salt, pepper, paprika, and garlic powder.
3. Place in a roasting pan and cover with foil. Roast for 3-4 hours.
4. Simmer bourbon, brown sugar, vinegar, and broth until thickened.
5. Glaze the brisket and roast uncovered for another 30 minutes.

Cranberry-Stuffed Turkey Breast

Ingredients:

- 1 (3-4 lb) boneless turkey breast
- 1 cup dried cranberries
- ½ cup pecans, chopped
- 1 cup breadcrumbs
- 1 tsp sage
- 1 tsp thyme
- 1 tbsp butter
- ½ cup chicken broth

Instructions:

1. Preheat oven to 375°F (190°C).
2. Sauté cranberries, pecans, breadcrumbs, sage, and thyme in butter. Add broth to moisten.
3. Butterfly turkey breast and spread stuffing inside. Roll and tie with twine.
4. Roast for 45-60 minutes until internal temp reaches 165°F (74°C).

Korean BBQ Short Ribs

Ingredients:

- 2 lb beef short ribs (flanken-cut)
- ½ cup soy sauce
- ¼ cup brown sugar
- ¼ cup rice vinegar
- 2 tbsp sesame oil
- 4 cloves garlic, minced
- 1 tbsp grated ginger
- 1 tsp red pepper flakes

Instructions:

1. Mix all marinade ingredients and coat ribs. Marinate for at least 4 hours or overnight.
2. Grill over high heat for 3-4 minutes per side.
3. Serve with sesame seeds and green onions.

Marinated Roast Salmon

Ingredients:

- 1 (2 lb) salmon fillet
- ¼ cup white miso paste
- 2 tbsp soy sauce
- 2 tbsp mirin
- 1 tbsp honey
- 1 tbsp sesame oil

Instructions:

1. Mix miso, soy sauce, mirin, honey, and sesame oil.
2. Marinate salmon for 30 minutes.
3. Preheat oven to 400°F (200°C).
4. Roast for 12-15 minutes until flaky.

Peking Duck

Ingredients:

- 1 whole duck (5-6 lb)
- 2 tbsp honey
- 2 tbsp soy sauce
- 1 tbsp five-spice powder
- 1 tbsp salt
- 1 tsp baking powder

Instructions:

1. Mix honey, soy sauce, and five-spice powder. Rub onto duck.
2. Refrigerate uncovered overnight.
3. Preheat oven to 375°F (190°C). Roast for 2-2.5 hours.
4. Increase heat to 450°F (232°C) for the last 20 minutes to crisp the skin.

Maple Dijon Roasted Pork Loin

Ingredients:

- 1 (3-4 lb) pork loin
- 2 tbsp Dijon mustard
- ¼ cup maple syrup
- 1 tbsp apple cider vinegar
- 2 cloves garlic, minced
- 1 tsp rosemary

Instructions:

1. Preheat oven to 375°F (190°C).
2. Mix mustard, syrup, vinegar, garlic, and rosemary.
3. Rub onto pork and roast for 1-1.5 hours, basting occasionally, until internal temp reaches 145°F (63°C).
4. Rest for 10 minutes before slicing.

Citrus-Herb Roasted Sea Bass

Ingredients:

- 2 (6-8 oz) sea bass fillets
- 2 tbsp olive oil
- 1 lemon, sliced
- 1 orange, sliced
- 2 cloves garlic, minced
- 1 tbsp fresh thyme, chopped
- 1 tbsp fresh parsley, chopped
- 1 tsp salt
- ½ tsp black pepper

Instructions:

1. Preheat oven to 400°F (200°C).
2. Rub sea bass fillets with olive oil, garlic, thyme, parsley, salt, and pepper.
3. Place on a baking sheet with lemon and orange slices on top.
4. Roast for 12-15 minutes until the fish flakes easily.

Slow-Roasted Tomahawk Steak

Ingredients:

- 1 (2-3 lb) tomahawk ribeye steak
- 2 tbsp salt
- 1 tbsp black pepper
- 1 tbsp garlic powder
- 2 tbsp butter
- 2 cloves garlic, smashed
- 2 sprigs rosemary

Instructions:

1. Preheat oven to 250°F (120°C).
2. Season steak with salt, pepper, and garlic powder.
3. Place on a wire rack and roast for 1.5-2 hours until internal temp reaches 120°F (49°C) for medium-rare.
4. Sear in a hot skillet with butter, garlic, and rosemary for 1-2 minutes per side.

Char Siu (Chinese BBQ Pork)

Ingredients:

- 2 lb pork shoulder, sliced into long strips
- ¼ cup hoisin sauce
- ¼ cup honey
- ¼ cup soy sauce
- 2 tbsp Shaoxing wine
- 1 tsp five-spice powder
- 1 tsp red food coloring (optional)
- 2 cloves garlic, minced

Instructions:

1. Mix all marinade ingredients and coat pork. Marinate for at least 4 hours or overnight.
2. Preheat oven to 375°F (190°C).
3. Roast for 40-50 minutes, basting every 15 minutes.
4. Broil for 2-3 minutes to caramelize.

Coffee-Rubbed Prime Rib

Ingredients:

- 1 (4-6 lb) prime rib roast
- 2 tbsp ground coffee
- 1 tbsp kosher salt
- 1 tbsp black pepper
- 1 tsp smoked paprika
- 1 tsp garlic powder
- 1 tsp brown sugar

Instructions:

1. Mix coffee, salt, pepper, paprika, garlic powder, and brown sugar.
2. Rub onto the roast and let sit for 1 hour.
3. Preheat oven to 450°F (232°C). Roast for 20 minutes.
4. Reduce heat to 325°F (163°C) and cook until internal temp reaches 130°F (54°C) for medium-rare.
5. Rest for 20 minutes before slicing.

Mustard-Crusted Roast Lamb

Ingredients:

- 1 (4-5 lb) bone-in leg of lamb
- 3 tbsp Dijon mustard
- 2 tbsp olive oil
- 2 tbsp fresh rosemary, chopped
- 2 cloves garlic, minced
- 1 tsp salt
- ½ tsp black pepper

Instructions:

1. Preheat oven to 375°F (190°C).
2. Mix mustard, olive oil, rosemary, garlic, salt, and pepper. Rub onto lamb.
3. Roast for 1.5-2 hours until internal temp reaches 135°F (57°C) for medium-rare.

Balsamic Glazed Roast Quail

Ingredients:

- 4 whole quail
- 2 tbsp olive oil
- ¼ cup balsamic vinegar
- 2 tbsp honey
- 2 cloves garlic, minced
- 1 tsp thyme
- 1 tsp salt
- ½ tsp black pepper

Instructions:

1. Preheat oven to 400°F (200°C).
2. Mix balsamic vinegar, honey, garlic, thyme, salt, and pepper. Rub onto quail.
3. Roast for 20-25 minutes, basting with glaze every 10 minutes.

Rosemary Garlic Roasted Venison

Ingredients:

- 2 lb venison roast
- 2 tbsp olive oil
- 2 tbsp fresh rosemary, chopped
- 2 cloves garlic, minced
- 1 tsp salt
- ½ tsp black pepper

Instructions:

1. Preheat oven to 375°F (190°C).
2. Rub venison with olive oil, rosemary, garlic, salt, and pepper.
3. Roast for 30-40 minutes until internal temp reaches 130°F (54°C) for medium-rare.

Indian-Spiced Roast Goat

Ingredients:

- 3 lb goat leg
- 2 tbsp yogurt
- 2 tbsp garam masala
- 1 tbsp turmeric
- 1 tbsp cumin
- 1 tbsp coriander
- 1 tbsp ginger paste
- 1 tbsp garlic paste
- 1 tsp salt
- ½ tsp black pepper

Instructions:

1. Mix all spices with yogurt and rub onto the goat. Marinate for at least 4 hours.
2. Preheat oven to 325°F (163°C).
3. Roast for 2.5-3 hours until tender.

Applewood Smoked Pork Shoulder

Ingredients:

- 1 (5-6 lb) pork shoulder
- 2 tbsp salt
- 1 tbsp black pepper
- 1 tbsp smoked paprika
- 1 tbsp brown sugar
- 1 tsp garlic powder
- 1 tsp onion powder

Instructions:

1. Rub pork with spices and let sit for 1 hour.
2. Set smoker to 225°F (107°C) with applewood chips.
3. Smoke for 8-10 hours until internal temp reaches 195°F (90°C).

Five-Spice Roasted Duck

Ingredients:

- 1 whole duck (5-6 lb)
- 2 tbsp soy sauce
- 1 tbsp five-spice powder
- 1 tbsp honey
- 1 tsp salt
- 1 tsp baking powder

Instructions:

1. Mix soy sauce, five-spice powder, honey, salt, and baking powder. Rub onto duck.
2. Refrigerate uncovered overnight.
3. Preheat oven to 375°F (190°C). Roast for 2-2.5 hours.
4. Increase heat to 450°F (232°C) for the last 20 minutes to crisp the skin.

Chimichurri Roasted Tri-Tip

Ingredients:

- 2 lb tri-tip roast
- 2 tbsp olive oil
- 1 tbsp salt
- 1 tsp black pepper
- 1 tsp smoked paprika
- 1 tsp garlic powder

Chimichurri Sauce:

- ½ cup fresh parsley, chopped
- ¼ cup fresh cilantro, chopped
- 3 cloves garlic, minced
- 2 tbsp red wine vinegar
- ½ cup olive oil
- 1 tsp red pepper flakes
- Salt and pepper to taste

Instructions:

1. Preheat oven to 400°F (200°C).
2. Rub tri-tip with olive oil, salt, pepper, paprika, and garlic powder.
3. Roast for 25-30 minutes until internal temp reaches 130°F (54°C) for medium-rare.
4. Let rest for 10 minutes before slicing.
5. Mix all chimichurri ingredients and serve over sliced tri-tip.

Herb Butter Roasted Cornish Hen

Ingredients:

- 2 Cornish hens
- 4 tbsp butter, softened
- 2 cloves garlic, minced
- 1 tbsp fresh rosemary, chopped
- 1 tbsp fresh thyme, chopped
- 1 tsp salt
- ½ tsp black pepper
- 1 lemon, halved

Instructions:

1. Preheat oven to 425°F (218°C).
2. Mix butter, garlic, rosemary, thyme, salt, and pepper.
3. Rub mixture under and over the skin of the hens.
4. Place lemon halves inside the cavity.
5. Roast for 40-50 minutes until internal temp reaches 165°F (74°C).

Tandoori Spiced Roast Chicken

Ingredients:

- 1 whole chicken (4-5 lb)
- 1 cup plain yogurt
- 2 tbsp lemon juice
- 1 tbsp garam masala
- 1 tbsp paprika
- 1 tbsp cumin
- 1 tbsp coriander
- 1 tsp turmeric
- 1 tsp salt
- 1 tsp black pepper
- 2 cloves garlic, minced
- 1 tbsp grated ginger

Instructions:

1. Mix yogurt, lemon juice, and spices. Rub over chicken and marinate for 4 hours or overnight.
2. Preheat oven to 375°F (190°C).
3. Roast for 1.5-2 hours until internal temp reaches 165°F (74°C).

Szechuan Peppercorn Beef Roast

Ingredients:

- 3 lb beef roast (ribeye or sirloin)
- 1 tbsp Szechuan peppercorns, crushed
- 1 tbsp salt
- 1 tbsp soy sauce
- 1 tbsp hoisin sauce
- 1 tbsp rice vinegar
- 1 tbsp honey
- 2 cloves garlic, minced

Instructions:

1. Preheat oven to 350°F (175°C).
2. Mix all seasonings into a paste and rub onto the beef.
3. Roast for 1.5-2 hours until internal temp reaches 130°F (54°C) for medium-rare.

Black Garlic Roasted Turkey

Ingredients:

- 1 (12-14 lb) turkey
- 6 cloves black garlic, mashed
- 4 tbsp butter, softened
- 2 tbsp soy sauce
- 1 tbsp honey
- 1 tbsp fresh thyme, chopped
- 1 tsp salt
- ½ tsp black pepper

Instructions:

1. Preheat oven to 325°F (163°C).
2. Mix butter, black garlic, soy sauce, honey, thyme, salt, and pepper.
3. Rub under and over the turkey skin.
4. Roast for 3-4 hours, basting every 30 minutes, until internal temp reaches 165°F (74°C).

Maple Bourbon Glazed Salmon

Ingredients:

- 1 (2 lb) salmon fillet
- ¼ cup maple syrup
- 2 tbsp bourbon
- 1 tbsp Dijon mustard
- 1 tbsp soy sauce
- 1 tsp garlic powder

Instructions:

1. Mix maple syrup, bourbon, mustard, soy sauce, and garlic powder.
2. Marinate salmon for 30 minutes.
3. Preheat oven to 400°F (200°C).
4. Roast for 12-15 minutes until flaky.

Braised and Roasted Oxtail

Ingredients:

- 3 lb oxtail
- 2 tbsp olive oil
- 1 onion, chopped
- 2 carrots, chopped
- 2 cloves garlic, minced
- 2 cups beef broth
- 1 cup red wine
- 2 sprigs thyme
- 1 bay leaf
- 1 tsp salt
- ½ tsp black pepper

Instructions:

1. Preheat oven to 325°F (163°C).
2. Sear oxtail in olive oil until browned. Remove from pot.
3. Sauté onion, carrots, and garlic until soft.
4. Add broth, wine, thyme, bay leaf, salt, and pepper. Return oxtail to pot.
5. Cover and braise in oven for 3 hours until tender.
6. Uncover and roast at 400°F (200°C) for 20 minutes for a crispy exterior.

Cajun Spiced Roast Pork

Ingredients:

- 3 lb pork loin
- 2 tbsp olive oil
- 1 tbsp smoked paprika
- 1 tbsp garlic powder
- 1 tbsp onion powder
- 1 tsp cayenne pepper
- 1 tsp dried oregano
- 1 tsp dried thyme
- 1 tsp salt
- ½ tsp black pepper

Instructions:

1. Preheat oven to 375°F (190°C).
2. Mix spices and rub onto pork.
3. Roast for 1-1.5 hours until internal temp reaches 145°F (63°C).
4. Let rest for 10 minutes before slicing.

Brown Sugar Glazed Meatloaf

Ingredients:

- 2 lb ground beef
- 1 cup breadcrumbs
- 1 small onion, finely chopped
- 2 cloves garlic, minced
- 1 egg
- ½ cup milk
- 1 tbsp Worcestershire sauce
- 1 tsp salt
- ½ tsp black pepper

Glaze:

- ½ cup brown sugar
- ¼ cup ketchup
- 1 tbsp Dijon mustard

Instructions:

1. Preheat oven to 375°F (190°C).
2. Mix all meatloaf ingredients and shape into a loaf. Place in a baking dish.
3. Mix glaze ingredients and spread over meatloaf.
4. Bake for 1 hour until internal temp reaches 160°F (71°C).

Soy-Ginger Glazed Roast Goose

Ingredients:

- 1 whole goose (10-12 lb)
- ¼ cup soy sauce
- 2 tbsp honey
- 1 tbsp fresh ginger, grated
- 2 cloves garlic, minced
- 1 tbsp rice vinegar
- 1 tsp five-spice powder

Instructions:

1. Preheat oven to 350°F (175°C).
2. Mix glaze ingredients and rub over the goose.
3. Roast for 2.5-3 hours, basting every 30 minutes.
4. Let rest for 15 minutes before carving.

French Onion Roasted Ribeye

Ingredients:

- 1 (3-4 lb) ribeye roast
- 2 tbsp olive oil
- 2 large onions, caramelized
- 3 cloves garlic, minced
- 1 cup beef broth
- 1 tbsp Worcestershire sauce
- 1 tsp salt
- ½ tsp black pepper
- ½ tsp thyme

Instructions:

1. Preheat oven to 400°F (200°C).
2. Sear ribeye in olive oil, then place in a roasting pan.
3. Top with caramelized onions and pour broth and Worcestershire sauce over.
4. Roast for 45-60 minutes until internal temp reaches 130°F (54°C) for medium-rare.

Roasted Bison Sirloin

Ingredients:

- 2 lb bison sirloin
- 2 tbsp olive oil
- 1 tbsp fresh rosemary, chopped
- 2 cloves garlic, minced
- 1 tsp salt
- ½ tsp black pepper

Instructions:

1. Preheat oven to 375°F (190°C).
2. Rub bison with olive oil, rosemary, garlic, salt, and pepper.
3. Roast for 25-30 minutes until internal temp reaches 130°F (54°C) for medium-rare.

Pistachio Crusted Rack of Lamb

Ingredients:

- 1 (2 lb) rack of lamb
- ½ cup pistachios, finely chopped
- 2 tbsp Dijon mustard
- 1 tbsp honey
- 2 tbsp olive oil
- 1 tsp salt
- ½ tsp black pepper

Instructions:

1. Preheat oven to 400°F (200°C).
2. Mix pistachios, mustard, honey, olive oil, salt, and pepper.
3. Coat the lamb with the mixture.
4. Roast for 20-25 minutes until internal temp reaches 130°F (54°C) for medium-rare.

Hoisin-Glazed Roast Duck

Ingredients:

- 1 whole duck (5-6 lb)
- ¼ cup hoisin sauce
- 2 tbsp soy sauce
- 1 tbsp honey
- 1 tbsp rice vinegar
- 1 tsp five-spice powder

Instructions:

1. Preheat oven to 375°F (190°C).
2. Mix glaze ingredients and rub over the duck.
3. Roast for 2-2.5 hours, basting every 30 minutes.

Garlic Rosemary Roasted Wild Boar

Ingredients:

- 3 lb wild boar roast
- 3 cloves garlic, minced
- 2 tbsp fresh rosemary, chopped
- 2 tbsp olive oil
- 1 tsp salt
- ½ tsp black pepper

Instructions:

1. Preheat oven to 350°F (175°C).
2. Rub boar with garlic, rosemary, olive oil, salt, and pepper.
3. Roast for 1.5-2 hours until internal temp reaches 145°F (63°C).

Argentine Asado Beef Roast

Ingredients:

- 3 lb beef roast (ribeye or sirloin)
- 2 tbsp coarse salt
- 1 tbsp black pepper
- 1 tbsp olive oil

Chimichurri Sauce:

- ½ cup fresh parsley, chopped
- ¼ cup fresh oregano, chopped
- 3 cloves garlic, minced
- 2 tbsp red wine vinegar
- ½ cup olive oil
- 1 tsp red pepper flakes

Instructions:

1. Preheat oven to 250°F (120°C).
2. Rub beef with salt, pepper, and olive oil.
3. Slow-roast for 2-3 hours until internal temp reaches 130°F (54°C) for medium-rare.
4. Rest for 10 minutes and serve with chimichurri.

Cherry Balsamic Glazed Roast Chicken

Ingredients:

- 1 whole chicken (4-5 lb)
- ½ cup cherry preserves
- ¼ cup balsamic vinegar
- 1 tbsp honey
- 1 tsp salt
- ½ tsp black pepper

Instructions:

1. Preheat oven to 375°F (190°C).
2. Mix glaze ingredients and brush over chicken.
3. Roast for 1.5-2 hours, basting every 30 minutes.

Pomegranate Molasses Roasted Lamb

Ingredients:

- 4 lb lamb leg
- ¼ cup pomegranate molasses
- 2 tbsp olive oil
- 1 tbsp fresh mint, chopped
- 2 cloves garlic, minced
- 1 tsp salt
- ½ tsp black pepper

Instructions:

1. Preheat oven to 375°F (190°C).
2. Mix pomegranate molasses, olive oil, mint, garlic, salt, and pepper.
3. Rub onto lamb and roast for 1.5-2 hours until internal temp reaches 135°F (57°C) for medium-rare.

Truffle Butter Roasted Filet Mignon

Ingredients:

- 4 (6 oz) filet mignon steaks
- 2 tbsp truffle butter
- 1 tbsp olive oil
- 1 tsp salt
- ½ tsp black pepper
- 2 cloves garlic, minced
- 1 sprig fresh thyme

Instructions:

1. Preheat oven to 400°F (200°C).
2. Season filets with salt and pepper.
3. Heat olive oil in a skillet over high heat and sear steaks for 2 minutes per side.
4. Transfer to oven and roast for 5-7 minutes for medium-rare.
5. Top with truffle butter and let rest for 5 minutes before serving.

Smoked Paprika Roasted Pork Ribs

Ingredients:

- 2 racks baby back ribs
- 2 tbsp smoked paprika
- 1 tbsp brown sugar
- 1 tbsp garlic powder
- 1 tsp salt
- ½ tsp black pepper
- 1 cup BBQ sauce

Instructions:

1. Preheat oven to 300°F (150°C).
2. Mix paprika, brown sugar, garlic powder, salt, and pepper. Rub onto ribs.
3. Wrap ribs in foil and bake for 2.5-3 hours.
4. Brush with BBQ sauce and broil for 5 minutes for a caramelized finish.

Lebanese Spiced Roast Leg of Lamb

Ingredients:

- 4 lb leg of lamb
- 2 tbsp olive oil
- 1 tbsp ground cumin
- 1 tbsp ground coriander
- 1 tbsp ground allspice
- 1 tsp cinnamon
- 1 tsp salt
- ½ tsp black pepper
- 3 cloves garlic, minced
- Juice of 1 lemon

Instructions:

1. Preheat oven to 375°F (190°C).
2. Mix all spices, garlic, lemon juice, and olive oil. Rub onto lamb.
3. Roast for 1.5-2 hours until internal temp reaches 135°F (57°C) for medium-rare.

Harissa Roasted Chicken

Ingredients:

- 1 whole chicken (4-5 lb)
- ¼ cup harissa paste
- 2 tbsp olive oil
- 1 tsp ground cumin
- 1 tsp smoked paprika
- 1 tsp salt
- ½ tsp black pepper
- Juice of 1 lemon

Instructions:

1. Preheat oven to 375°F (190°C).
2. Mix harissa, olive oil, cumin, paprika, salt, pepper, and lemon juice.
3. Rub over chicken and roast for 1.5-2 hours, basting occasionally.

Plum-Glazed Roast Pheasant

Ingredients:

- 2 whole pheasants
- ½ cup plum preserves
- 2 tbsp balsamic vinegar
- 1 tbsp soy sauce
- 1 tsp fresh thyme, chopped
- 1 clove garlic, minced
- 1 tsp salt
- ½ tsp black pepper

Instructions:

1. Preheat oven to 375°F (190°C).
2. Mix plum preserves, vinegar, soy sauce, thyme, garlic, salt, and pepper.
3. Brush onto pheasants and roast for 50-60 minutes, basting occasionally.

Saffron and Orange Roasted Quail

Ingredients:

- 4 whole quail
- ¼ cup orange juice
- 1 tbsp honey
- 1 tbsp olive oil
- ¼ tsp saffron threads
- 1 clove garlic, minced
- 1 tsp salt
- ½ tsp black pepper

Instructions:

1. Preheat oven to 400°F (200°C).
2. Mix orange juice, honey, olive oil, saffron, garlic, salt, and pepper.
3. Rub over quail and roast for 15-20 minutes.

Fig and Port Wine Roasted Venison

Ingredients:

- 2 lb venison loin
- ½ cup port wine
- ¼ cup fig preserves
- 2 tbsp balsamic vinegar
- 1 tbsp olive oil
- 1 tsp salt
- ½ tsp black pepper
- 1 sprig rosemary

Instructions:

1. Preheat oven to 375°F (190°C).
2. Mix port wine, fig preserves, balsamic vinegar, olive oil, salt, and pepper.
3. Rub onto venison and roast for 25-30 minutes until internal temp reaches 130°F (54°C) for medium-rare.

www.ingramcontent.com/pod-product-compliance
Lightning Source LLC
LaVergne TN
LVHW061954070526
838199LV00060B/4110